How to Be Social

A Guide to Talking to People with Comfort, Confidence, and Ease

by Kathleen Bishopson

Table of Contents

Introduction

If you naturally have an introverted personality, you may find every excuse to skip the party. You just simply don't enjoy meeting new people or making an effort to carry on conversation, even with people you already know. Maybe you've even started to convince yourself that you just enjoy your own company more, and prefer to be alone.

Most of the time, people actually have a poor social life because of other underlying issues like low self-esteem and low-to-no self-confidence. This book offers a holistic outlook on why you are not as social as you could or should be. In this Guide, you'll learn how to become more social, and how to make sociability a regular part of your lifestyle. To do this, you don't need professional help. You just need to read on, and invest a little time and effort, and soon your social life will take off beautifully. And guess what: you'll actually enjoy it!

Life is too short to spend it lonely, gloomy, and miserable. Life should be enjoyed, it should be lived fully, which includes meeting new people and making friends. You see, your destiny in life is *too BIG* for you to achieve it alone. You need the support of other people and you need to offer your support to others too. Sadly, you can't do any of this if your only companion is your Smartphone.

Do you think that it's other people who don't want to talk to you? Well then, you think wrong. People actually want an excuse to talk a lot, especially about themselves. They just want you to get them started, to make them feel good about themselves, and then they'll tell you more than you bargained for.

How do you view yourself? Do you like what you see in your own mind about yourself? Do you think you are confident? "*As a man thinks, so he is*," the saying goes. If you think you need more social life, then you do. If you think you need more confidence, then you do. On the other hand, if you think you are social, then you are. And if you think you are confident, then you are! I'll explain how to change your mindset later.

The first step towards a solution is to admit to yourself that indeed, you do need to get out there more often, make more friends, meet new people, and so on. This book will help you realize all these goals.

Confidence and good Social Skills can win you jobs, more friends, and even lovers (if that's what you're looking for). Believe me, when you have a good social life, you will get plenty of assurance and self-confidence back. You can be more assertive, more confident, and people will respect you tremendously.

Chapter 1 - How to Start Being Social

When you find that you are not good with people, have to hunt for words, and you usually prefer to keep to yourself, then most likely, whether you realize it or not: Your confidence takes a dive and you lose your assertiveness.

A social person is an individual who enjoys mingling and sharing with others in terms of ideologies, humor, and approach towards life. A social person genuinely likes the company of others and does not put up a charade to please those around him or her. There are many ways of becoming a social individual and for starters; it is important for you to first work out your inner issues. Your low self-esteem could be derailing you from being a social individual.

Everyone, even those who are shy, wants to be able to easily meet new people and strike up conversation. But how do you go about it? For starters, you have to accept that you are an introvert and that you can use a boost in your level of self-confidence. Second, you have to be interested. And why shouldn't you be interested? People are the most interesting part of this world! If these two factors are covered, then you are on the road to becoming a very social person. The upcoming advice on how to become a social person must be approached with your willingness to try to generally carry yourself as a friendly and social individual.

Here are a few tips on how to socialize easily

Here's a trick to start that will work wonders almost instantly: Keep things simple. Hold your head up high (chin up), look others directly in the eye with a slight/pleasant smile on your face, and give firm handshakes as you're meeting and mingling with others. At first, this might feel forced. But the beauty of it is that the more you do it, the more natural it becomes. It's like riding a bike. Just get through that first uncomfortable, scary, and wobbly part, and once you get the hang of it – there's no looking back. You will now forever know how to ride a bike (or in this case: smile with your chin up, while make eye contact, and shake someone's hand firmly) and it will feel natural thereafter.

Other simple ways of becoming social include the following:

Be Updated

Not on gossip, but on matters of current events, movies, fashion, sports, and more constructive stories. Ignorance and negligence are the enemies of socialization. Read a book, a magazine, the dailies, or at least watch the news on TV. Stay abreast with both local and international news. This way, you'll start to feel more confident in your ability to hold a healthy conversation.

Look and Smell Good

Neat people are always more confident, and more prepared to go out there and strike up a conversation. If you are well groomed, you will not be wondering about people's perception of you in the middle of a conversation.

Learn to Listen, and Listen to Learn

A lot of people listen only in order to keep the conversation flowing, or figure out what they're going to say next. But what if you actually listened to understand? The conversation would be more interesting and less redundant. Also, those around you will respect you more, because it will be apparent that you're not being social in a shallow way, rather you're there to get something meaningful out of conversation.

Don't Be a Sycophant

Don't be someone who just nods along and says yes to everything. Have your own perspective, and agree to disagree occasionally. It is healthy, and others will respect that, especially if you can disagree in a polite manner while still acknowledging the other person's perspective and its legitimacy.

Right Conversation, Wrong Crowd

There is a time and place for everything, therefore there's no specific rule for conversation and topics you should choose or avoid. However, keep in mind, the conversation that might appeal to your peers or classmates might not necessarily appeal to an older relative or colleague. Avoid discussing emotive topics such as religion and politics with strangers. Or if you must, then at least get to know their affiliation before delving into such topics, and be respectful of their right to have an opinion the same way you have a right to yours.

Read the Mood

Mood readers are known as those with good "social awareness." They always win because they understand that timing is everything. For example, if you approach a group of people standing around chatting, try to pick up on the mood before busting out that joke you just heard on Comedy Central. You never know what was just being discussed – it's possible that someone just finished explaining that her sister was recently diagnosed with terminal cancer, and you completely missed the give-away somber look on everyone's face. So always take a moment to pick up on the mood, this sensibility will serve you well.

Be Well-Rounded

If you intend to be a social person, consider being an all-round conversationalist. Matters including the economy, fashion, box office, billboard charts, government policies, sports, and much more, are most likely to make the material for conversation. You do not need to be an expert in any of these fields; just try to be at least a step above completely clueless, and you'll manage just fine.

Ask Pertinent Questions

This is by far my number one and favorite tip, and my secret tool, especially when I feel particularly ignorant about a certain topic. You don't want to just stand there, silent, while others carry on the conversation around you, do you? But on the other hand, you really don't have anything to contribute. So what do you do?

That's easy – just start asking intelligent and pertinent questions! Here's an example: I'm not much of a basketball fan, but my husband is, and his friends are. So when we're all together and they're discussing basketball, here's what I don't do. I don't sit there like a dud without contributing to the conversation – that would be awkward and make me feel pretty lame. I don't try to change the subject to something I'm more comfortable with – that would be rude and inconsiderate. And I don't just get up and walk away – again that would be rude, not to mention it would be a missed opportunity to learn a thing or two. Instead, I listen carefully to what's being discussed, and I ask intelligent questions every now and then that are pertinent in that very moment.

If they're talking about whether or not the Miami Heat will win the National Championship, then I might ask "When's the last time the Heat won?" or "Who's the favored team this year?" Then, while the guys happily answer my question, their answers also usually carry their own conversation to a new direction they may not have expected, which is enjoyable for them as well. They might say "Well, the Heat's not favored to win this year – the Spurs are. But if the Heat loses in the finals, they'll get a better draft pick. I bet they'll try to get that guy from So-and-So College who's supposed to be pretty unbelievable." Then, the next person would chime in "Oh yeah, that guy was a freshman all-star, and has since led his college to victory for the past 3 years. He's such an incredible player and he would actually pair well with LeBron James if Miami picked him up." Now, if you know anything about Basketball, you can probably tell I'm making this particular conversation up entirely. But, the tactic itself is incredibly useful. I have managed to be a part of the conversation without have any initial knowledge on the topic; I have managed to learn something about basketball – and learning is always a good thing; and I have shown to my husband and his friends that I can be easygoing and well-rounded or interested enough in any topic to be a part of a conversation.

So next time you're standing around, listening to people talk about something that you have no knowledge or interest in, just try to have a good attitude, ask a few questions, and be open-minded to learning a thing or two. This is a huge part of socialization.

Chapter 2 - What is Shyness, and How to Overcome it?

Shyness is probably one of the least-discussed topics under the sun. You have seen people who blush every time they look someone in the eyes. Maybe you are one of them, wishing that the earth would open up and swallow you up rather than have to face a person face to face. Or maybe you are shy and you don't even know it.

There is nothing wrong with being shy. Many men will tell you that they prefer shy girls. However, shyness is a tad too restricting when you cannot contribute to conversations or debates, or when your confidence takes flight out the window whenever you meet strangers, or when your self esteem takes a dip as you stand in front of people. If you cannot face a panel of interviewers, and look them in the eyes, how do you expect to win that job?

If you are shy, you are not alone because occasionally, everyone gets a little shy, especially when in the presence of strangers. There are various types of shyness. For instance, there are people that feel shy when they are addressing a huge crowd, others feel shy when they spot a very attractive person, while some feel shy in the presence of strangers, colleagues, or their seniors.

Have you ever taken a minute to ponder on what shyness is all about? Is it a psychological problem, or is it just a meaningless awkward feeling? According to psychologists, shyness is actually an emotion that determines an individual's behavior. In some instances, shyness is perceived as an anti-social behavior that can affect relationships with the people around you, potential employers/clients, a potential mate and so much more. Shy people sometimes even unintentionally come across as snobs or as people with a bad attitude.

Indications that you are shy

Everyone goes through bouts of shyness at some point in their life. Studies indicate that 45% of adults in America are actually shy. Shyness manifests itself in so many forms, for example:

- Difficulty maintaining eye contact
- Feeling insecure, nervous, or timid
- Feeling self-conscious and unsure of yourself
- Speechlessness
- Blushing and palm sweating
- Feeling breathless and shaky
- Feeling humiliation
- Aloofness and detachment

You tend to feel shy when your brain's lower levels are trying to shield you from a perception that is interpreted by your brain as a threat, making you feeling inferior when you compare yourself with those around you.

According to a poll conducted among the American youth, this mostly happens when you face a person you perceive as 'overly' attractive. In such a situation, you might struggle to conjure a conversation and end up sounding awkward because you are busy wondering what this person thinks of you.

A shy person's brain looks at the world from a different point of view as compared to an extrovert. Scientifically, shyness is a personality trait that is also known as SPS (Sensory Perception Sensitivity). SPS is common in children brought up in harsh environments (for example: parents yelling at them regularly, irrational punishment, spanking by adults, and bullying at school). Such children tend to warm up very slowly. They keep to themselves, get defensive and cry easily.

Shy individuals are known to be keen on detail. They are sensitive and their brains are hyperactive as compared to extroverts. Additionally, introverts/shy individuals tend to be very creative because their brain is always processing visual information.

Chapter 3 - How to be more Social, more Confident, and Friendlier

In the first chapter, we looked at how you can start to become social. The whole idea about enhancing your social life is to get more people to interact with you and like you. When people like you, you can build your self-confidence and with that, many doors will open. Here are some of the changes you will see:

- A great social life can open many career, life, and even marriage opportunities for you.

- If you are too shy, people might think you have an attitude, and they will tend to distance themselves from you.

- There is only so much fun that you can have alone.

- Failure to address your poor social life could have dire repercussions, for example: not getting married, missing job opportunities, being sad or lonely, missing out on fun, and much more, that would eventually lead to feelings of self-pity, stress, and depression.

10 Tips to Help you Socialize Easily

Be Natural

Unnatural people often come across as hypocrites and no one wants to associate with such. Also, avoid over-analyzing an interaction session because this might hold you back from becoming better and more relaxed. It is natural to anticipate the next meeting but it is also important to ensure that you do not go overboard with your analysis.

One Step at a Time

Don't rush things. Instead, tackle each moment as it comes. If you intend to be more social at the work place, you can start with a simple hello, a smile, and eye contact before jumping into heavy discussions with your fellow colleagues.

Be Brief and Concise

Do not start speaking fluff in the name of prolonging a conversation. Make it simple, direct, and to the point. You have plenty of important and valuable things to talk about, so don't dilute yourself by speaking just to fill silence with empty words.

Radiate Positive Energy

You will be amazed at how people respond to, and appreciate hanging around, people who radiate positive energy.

It's Never That Serious

Avoid focusing on what might go wrong. Focus on what might go right instead. Do not let a bitter past experience cloud your present moment, because everyone goes through a faux pas occasionally. Therefore, if once-upon-a-time things did not go as planned, don't let it haunt you and spoil your present time. Goofing up is part of the learning process after all.

Don't be Shy to Display your Gifts & Talents

Highlighting your talents boosts your confidence psychologically, which allows you to shine. If you are good at painting or photography, don't be too shy to mention something about these topics. (Obviously come up with something more tactful or modest than "Hey, guess what? I'm an amazing painter!"). By being able to modestly highlight your skills and talents, you will not only impress, but you will also open floodgates of opportunities and endless possibilities.

Be Eager to Learn

Even as you show others your talents, do not be a know-it-all because there is someone out there who knows something that you probably don't. It is not a bad thing to learn a little something from others. The world is a classroom and we must be willing to learn in order to increase our knowledge. Don't let pride or ego lead you to believe that you are the only one in the room with any knowledge or information to offer.

Be your Own Person

Nothing is as off-putting as an individual who doesn't have his/her own identity. Be firm on the things that you are willing to compromise on, and those that are off-limits for you. People around you will respect you for that.

Do not Discriminate

One of the fastest ways to become social is by mingling with people from different backgrounds. Avoid prejudice and stereotyping because this is a sure way to miss some amazing people and life lessons. Every person has innate goodness in them, and can add some value to your life. Look for goodness in people, and be open minded.

Chapter 4 – Although you're an Introvert, Break out of the Cocoon!

Being an introvert is not really a bad thing. In any case, even the most outgoing of extroverts find that at one time or another, they need some time to themselves so they can listen to their inner voice. However, being very comfortable as an introvert can have its limitations too and they can be dire. For example, you could even miss catching the spouse of your dreams. Now that'd be a terrible loss, right?

Most introverts know that they are introverts and they love their company more than they love that of other people. However, in most cases, they do feel a bit lonely which is why you may be looking for ways to be more social. Luckily, this isn't too hard. Of course, it won't happen overnight, but here are some tips to help make the adjustment easier:

Start by forming casual friendships

Most introverts find it difficult to form close friendships. Therefore, it is advised to start by forming casual friendships. Close friendship can be overwhelming, you know, with people telling you their dreams, expectations of life and so forth and expecting you to reciprocate. If you start by trying to make close friends, you could end up plunging into the depths of introversion again because you think that your privacy is at risk.

To make friendships easily with people, you may have to take some time to learn about them, and their friendship preferences. You see, some people look for close friendship all the time and therefore won't be very compatible with you. Don't worry too much if you don't seem to make friends as fast as you would like. It is only natural that you will like some people and dislike some, without any due reason. Take it easy, take your time.

Set up a social follow-up program for every week

After you take the first step of having met someone and thus formed a pretty simple or casual friendship, next, you must take other steps to ensure these friendships are nurtured to fruition, until they become close friendships. The good thing is it's really not that hard, if you are disciplined and organized. Why do we say disciplined? Because your natural instincts seem to only drive you away from people, rather than drive you towards people. It may take some effort from you, but eventually you will reap the rewards from it.

Create a simple routine of calling your new "casual" friends at least once a week. Later, you can make that twice or even thrice. Thanks to the advent of technology in communication, you can use various tools for catching up. You can text, email, use social networks, or simply pick up the phone. Eventually, your friends will start returning calls, and before you know it, communication will be regular.

Join a club

To start expanding your social circle, you'll want to add more friends. Joining a club actually makes this really easy. Through the club and its events, you'll be meeting new people all the time. At first, try joining one club and then sticking to it. The first few visits may seem awkward, like you're a guest, but once you've attended a few times in a row, you will start to feel more and more comfortable there. Once you make a new friend, fit them into your once-a-week follow-up routine.

Let your friendships grow

This is the fun part and after this stage, you will feel like an outgoing extrovert, with only short stints of introversion at times. By now, you already have a new close friend or two, and also quite a few casual friends. Friends will introduce you to their friends, and so on and so forth. By now, there may be too many to fit in your weekly follow up routine, but don't worry. That is how it was supposed to work out eventually.

Introduce your new friends to your old friends

You will find that it is much easier to keep in contact with friends who know each other than with friends who do not know each other. You'll be able to plan events, or meet and catch up with several of your friends at the same.

Chapter 5 - How to Start a Conversation and Keep it Going

In this chapter, we are going to try and turn you into a talker, where you can start and hold a conversation with a friend, or with anybody really. By now, you must have garnered some new social skills. Next, we're going to look at how to bring them into practice.

One of the primary bonds of friendship is communication. However, we are all wired differently when it comes to talking. Some of us can be quite chatty, while others of us are the silent type. However, one of the benchmarks of breaking out of your introversion cocoon is to ability to participate in conversation and to keep it going. Outloud. (Without being immersed in some imaginary conversation in your mind).

Conversation is a two way endeavor. There is a speaker and a listener. If one does too much talking, then it means that they did not take time to listen to what the other person was saying. If one does too much listening, then it might appear as if they aren't interested in the conversation.

To become good at conversation, you may need some practice. And you may also need to work on your listening skills. Note that I said "listening" and not "hearing" because the two verbs are different. Hearing just means that your ears are nearby; whereas Listening means that you heard it and that it was comprehended and evaluated in your mind. If you aren't a good listener, then you need to work on this ASAP. Practice by testing yourself post-conversation. What did that person say? See if you can answer this question, with specific details.

Here are a few communication skills that you should practice:

Balancing the Conversation

It is important that at the end of every conversation, you ask yourself just how much you talked. Whose voice was most dominant in the conversation? If you think that yours was heard more than your friend's was, it means that you had very little time to listen to what your friend was saying. One secret of giving the other person a lot of opportunity to speak is to ask a question after they tell you something. For example, if they tell you about their visit to the museum yesterday, you can say... "That sounds fun. What was your favorite exhibit?" That way, you will be encouraging them to talk some more about the event, rather than saying, "Oh, that sounds fun. I went to watch my brother play baseball yesterday."

When the other person is talking, you have to learn to add on their conversation rather than negate or ignore what they say. If they tell you about their bungee jumping experience, ask questions about it, or you can tell of a similar experience that you had some time back. Or you can mention how you would never bungee jump because it's too frightening for you. But always try to bring it back around and let them talk again. In these two examples, you could say "You bungee jumped in Australia? I bungee jumped once in Ireland. They tied the strap around my ankles. Did they do it that way with you in Australia too?" Or, "That's very brave of you. I'd be way too scared to try that, especially in a foreign country. Were you scared at all?"

See how I didn't steal or hijack the conversation away from them entirely? Instead, I interjected my own little piece, but then turned it back over to them with a follow-up question.

Practicing Chatting with your Office CoWorkers

And I don't mean instant messaging here, but try actually chatting live, in person, with people you work with in the office. This is a good opportunity to practice. Try choosing a subject that isn't too personal, but isn't work related. And definitely don't start gossiping about other coworkers or your boss. Just try making easy conversation, for example you could catch them in the office break room and start by asking what kind of tea they're making, noting that it smells really nice. Over time, conversation will evolve, and soon you may find someone who shares your interests and before you know it, you can start asking them to join you for lunch. The best thing is not to give up, even when you don't feel like talking.

Start conversations on a high note and end them on a high note

This is where a lot of people fail, by thinking that a sob story about their broken washing machine will get some sympathy listening. However, the truth is that most people have more than enough misery in their life and therefore they're just not interested in yours. Nobody likes a downer, a whiner, or a complainer. Be smart: Always start the conversation on a high note. For example, you can talk about a new restaurant in town you just tried that serves "the best garlic bread you've ever had," or about a new book that you have been reading, etc. Research shows that when you are more positive, people think of you as more likeable. Research also proves that at the founding stages, friendship cannot stand negativity.

Enhance your Self Image

Most introverts, though not all, have an inferiority complex. Therefore, the core of their problem is not really the introversion, but their low self-confidence and esteem. One sure thing however, is that if you are confident in yourself, other people will also be confident in you. If you show yourself some love, other people will be more inclined to like you. Introversion is a symptom. There is a root cause for it in most cases. Therefore, it is important that you work on treating the root causes of the inferiority complex so that you can get rid of the problem from its core source.

How do you feel about your wardrobe? Maybe you should revamp some things in your closet so as to feel better about the way you look. I say go ahead and do it! Look for the best in yourself, and once you find it, other people will find it.

Never defend yourself

Part of being social is feeling confident. And feeling confident means that you are sure of yourself, your choices, your statements, and your actions. If someone disagrees with something you've said or the way you've said it, trust me: just let it be. If you start to become defensive about your position, it's an easy give-away that you are insecure and not sure of yourself. Just remain calm, poised, and hold your chin up whether people agree with you or not. You will gain more respect this way, than by being defensive.

Do not put on an act for other people

Most shy people tend to want to hide that shyness from others. You are an introvert yes, but that is your personality and you don't have to justify it to anyone. However, having realized that you would be missing out on many things, the best thing to do is to start fighting your shyness rather than hide it from people.

Stop caring about comments regarding how much or how little you talk. The more you ignore these, the less they will affect you. Meanwhile you can invest more energy into practicing the rules of making great conversation that we have learned here.

Shyness is not an infection, a disease, a disorder, or an abnormality. The only thing it does, though, is make you miss out on many potentially fun moments with other people. You could be shy, however, and still have a great life too. However, always remember that opportunities come when you network with people, when you enlarge your social circles and so forth. Even when you are employed, you still need to participate in teamwork. That's why you need to get out of your comfort zone of introversion and start working on having a more active social life.

Chapter 6 - How to Become More Likeable & Regain Self-Confidence

A Universal Truth: All people love to be liked. When people are not liked by other people, they start feeling insecure, their self-esteem takes a dip, and out the window goes their self-confidence, their zeal and zest to fight in life and achieve their dreams.

Having learned how to become more social in past chapters, here, we will look at how you can become more likeable. If you have come out of your cocoon and started talking to people, including strangers, and started taking a more active interest in conversations happening around you, and made a bunch of friends and more, then consider the climatic goal here, which is to have people like you. It is a very rewarding experience, mostly because you too will start liking people in return.

Smile often

It doesn't matter how much or how little you talk, but if you're frequently smiling, it will say it all. They say that it's difficult to hate a person who smiles at you. There is such power in a smile. It draws people to you, people feel more comfortable and unless they are cuckoo, they will smile back at you. The reciprocation is automatic.

At the office, make a point of smiling to your colleagues before you say hi and then watch their reaction. They will smile back, but that is not the important thing. The most important thing is that when they smile back, you will feel so nice about it. After several such experiences, you will never want to pass anyone without smiling at them again.

Listen

Listen to people when they talk. And listen actively! Discern when people are just looking for someone to listen to them. This means that most times, people may be looking for someone to listen, not to necessarily offer them advice. People love people who can put a little time aside to listen to them. To encourage people to talk:

- Stop whatever you are doing to listen to them
- Look up, don't scroll through your phone as you listen to them
- Eye contact is paramount, and nodding along may help too
- Inject a question where you feel necessary
- Do not offer your advice or opinion unless it is asked for

Listening is not always easy, but with enough practice, you can muster and do it well every time.

Give compliments

Now that you've made a good number of friends, you want to treat them nicely so that they too can treat you in like manner. You also want them to like you. Everyone wants to feel good about themselves, and you can help them along that road. Having just come out of your introvert comfort zone, this may not be very easy.

Don't make ambiguous statements like... "You look good today." Rather, go for specifics. For example, you can compliment a lady on the blouse she is wearing. "That's a lovely blouse, blue looks great on you – it really brings out your eyes!" Just be careful not to overdo it, and of course don't say anything that's not somewhat true.

Like people

How did this one not make it to the top of this list? If you want people to like you, start by liking them! It is very hard to like people just for the sake of liking them, so try to think of what specific qualities make them unique and/or likeable. How do you show people that you like them without appearing pathetic? For one, we know that people usually like other people who like themselves and are confident. It's simple, so don't make rocket science out of something that's not. Just walk into a room, smile at somebody, and say "hi there," showing them that you acknowledge their existence and want to be friendly. They will then reciprocate, you'll see.

Humor makes people laugh

We are so engrossed in our careers nowadays, and take many things far too seriously, such that we don't leave much time to experience humor. Yet science shows that humor plays an integral part in our brain development and in the betterment of our life.

You will always love hanging out with people who can make you laugh. At work, most of the time, you will forget your love for laughter. It can be easy to create some humor at a party and laugh yourself silly, but it can be close to impossible to do the same at the traditional workplace where people don't even greet each other in the hallways, even though they work for the same firm. However, you can start by cracking a joke with your colleague. Or laugh at your own joke, even if they don't. Laughter is not only expensive, but it's also contagious. A few unashamed bouts of laughter and soon, others will join in. The thing to remember here is that people love hanging out with people that make them laugh.

Conclusion

Out of everything you've learned in this book, you have to remember this: It all starts with you. If you want others to be more social with you, then you must start by showing interest in them. If you want others to talk to you, then start by talking to them. If you want others to like you, then start by liking them.

Don't live in solitude anymore, with the mask of being an introvert and enjoying your own company more than others'. Man is a social creature, and you will limit yourself gravely if you don't make some changes in your patterns. Being social is a lifestyle, and once you start living this way, you'll never look back (except maybe to chuckle at yourself for being so shy and silly once upon a time). Try to think of socializing as a 'spark' that you want to keep going at all times because it makes life that much better. If you happen to hit a relapse, don't be hard on yourself, just remember how much more fun life is with other people in the mix.

Thank you for purchasing this book, and I really hope you found it helpful! If you enjoyed it, I'd really appreciate if you'd take a moment to leave a friendly review on Amazon. Thanks, and happy socializing!

Made in the USA
Middletown, DE
23 August 2020